GEORGE WASHINGTON CARVER

Teacher, Scientist, and Inventor

by LORI MORTENSEN

illustrated by NIAMH O'CONNOR

 PICTURE WINDOW BOOKS
Minneapolis, Minnesota

Special thanks to our advisers for their expertise:

Lois Brown, Ph.D.
Associate Professor, Department of English
American Studies Program and African American Studies Program
Mount Holyoke College, South Hadley, Massachusetts

Terry Flaherty, Ph.D.
Professor of English
Minnesota State University, Mankato

Editors: Jill Kalz and Shelly Lyons
Designer: Nathan Gassman
Page Production: Michelle Biedscheid
Associate Managing Editor: Christianne Jones
The illustrations in this book were created digitally and with pencil and ink.
Photo Credit: Library of Congress, page 3

Picture Window Books
5115 Excelsior Boulevard, Suite 232
Minneapolis, MN 55416
877-845-8392
www.picturewindowbooks.com

Printed in the United States of America.

All books published by Picture Window Books
are manufactured with paper containing at least
10 percent post-consumer waste.

Library of Congress Cataloging-in-Publication Data
Mortensen, Lori, 1955-
George Washington Carver : teacher, scientist, and inventor / by Lori Mortensen ;
illustrated by Niamh O'Connor.
p. cm.
ISBN-13: 978-1-4048-3725-6 (library binding)
ISBN-10: 1-4048-3725-6 (library binding)
1. Carver, George Washington, 1864?-1943—Juvenile literature. 2. Agriculturists—
United States—Biography—Juvenile literature. 3. African American agriculturists—
Biography—Juvenile literature. I. O'Connor, Niamh, ill. II. Title.
S417.C3M67 2007
630.92—dc22
[B]   2007004284

George Washington Carver was someone people looked up to. He overcame slavery and became a scientist. When poor black farmers could not grow cotton, George taught them how to grow peanuts. George became famous for finding new ways to use peanuts, but he never cared about money or fame. He committed his life to helping others.

This is the story of

George Washington Carver.

George Washington Carver was born around 1864 on a Missouri farm. George's parents were slaves. His father died in an accident before George was born. When George was a baby, slave stealers took George and his mother from their home. The two were separated, and George never saw his mother again.

Several weeks later, Missouri farmers Moses and Susan Carver found George and brought him back home. The Carvers, who disliked slavery even though they owned slaves, raised George as their son.

As a young boy, George loved plants. After doing chores, he often wandered through the woods and meadows. He wondered why some plants were small and others were tall. He wondered why some plants grew in the sun, while others grew in the shade. To find the answers, George grew a garden and did many experiments with soil, water, and sunshine.

By the time George was 8 years old, he knew a lot about plants. Neighbors called him "The Plant Doctor."

George loved to learn. He wanted to go to school but was not allowed to do so. At that time, the schools near his home were for white children only. When George was about 10 years old, he left home. He walked to a school for black children that was 8 miles (12.8 kilometers) away.

When George arrived at the school, a black couple took him in. He earned his keep by doing chores. After George learned all he could, he moved to another place and another school.

George continued studying plants and became an agricultural scientist. He taught at Iowa State College. The school had a laboratory and a greenhouse.

One day, George got a letter from Booker T. Washington. Booker was a former slave and the founder of a college in Alabama called Tuskegee Institute. He begged George to teach at his school. Booker said he had nothing to offer except hard work and a chance to help poor black farmers. George knew this was what he was meant to do.

11

George arrived at Tuskegee Institute in 1896. Everywhere he looked, the land was bare and wasted. Local farmers had grown cotton until the soil had worn out.

George taught students and the farmers who asked him for help. He showed them how to feed the soil and rotate crops. When the fields produced cotton again, the people cheered. Sadly, before the farmers could harvest the cotton, beetles ate the cotton plants. Nobody knew how to stop them.

George noticed that the beetles did not eat peanut plants. He told the farmers to grow peanuts instead.

When the farmers harvested the peanuts, however, nobody wanted to buy them. Peanuts were used only for hog feed.

George felt terrible about this mistake. He shut himself in his laboratory and did experiments around the clock. In only two days, George discovered peanuts were an amazing plant. Peanuts were good for making cooking oil, milk, cheese, and many other things.

George shared his discoveries about peanuts by inviting businessmen to a special lunch. He served soup, "chicken" loaf, vegetables, ice cream, and cookies. The guests enjoyed their meal.

16

Afterward, George told his guests that the lunch had been made from peanuts. As word spread about the amazing plant, people across the country began buying peanuts.

In time, George discovered more than 300 ways to use peanuts. He also found many ways to use cowpeas, sweet potatoes, soybeans, and cotton. One peanut product was used to treat thousands of people suffering from polio. Candy bars, peanut butter, dyes, cosmetics, inks, and much more could all be made from peanuts.

George's discoveries made him famous throughout the world. But he did not care about fame or money. He believed he was successful only if he helped others.

George Washington Carver died on January 5, 1943, at about 80 years of age. He was a true hero. He improved the way people farmed and helped millions of people make better lives for themselves.

The Life of George Washington Carver

1864	Born in Missouri; the exact date is unknown
1865	Slaves were freed at the end of the Civil War (1861–1865)
1874	Left home to go to school in Neosho, Missouri
1894	Graduated from Iowa State College and accepted a teaching position
1896	Received a letter from Booker T. Washington and taught at Tuskegee Institute in Tuskegee, Alabama
1903	Began finding uses for peanuts
1941	George Washington Carver Museum opened at Tuskegee Institute
1943	Died in Tuskegee, Alabama, on January 5, at about 80 years old
1943	President Franklin Delano Roosevelt dedicated a national monument in Missouri to George's memory; It was the first U.S national monument to honor an African American.

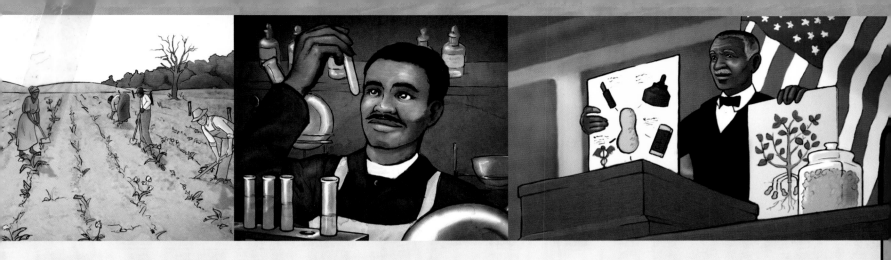

Did You Know?

~ George never married or had children.

~ George enjoyed painting pictures of the plants he loved. When he entered "Yucca and Cactus" in a statewide art contest in Iowa, his painting won first place.

~ George never accepted money for his discoveries. He said God had not charged him for his knowledge, so he would not, either.

~ When George arrived at Tuskegee Institute, he was given an empty room, a hoe, and a blind ox. George and his students collected old bottles, jars, and other things people had thrown away to use as laboratory equipment.

~ An important moment in George's life occurred in 1879, when he saw an African-American man pulled from jail and killed. At that moment, George decided he would do something to help all African Americans.

Glossary

agriculture — the science of growing crops

experiment — a scientific way of testing or exploring an idea

greenhouse — a glass building for growing plants

laboratory — a room used for experiments

polio — a disease caused by a virus that attacks the nervous system

rotate — to turn around; or growing crops in a certain order

slavery — the practice of owning people; slaves are not free and must do what their masters tell them to do

To Learn More

At the Library

Bowdish, Lynea. *George Washington Carver*. New York: Children's Press, 2004.

Carter, Andy and Carol Saller. *George Washington Carver*. Minneapolis: Carolrhoda Books, 2001.

Driscoll, Laura. *George Washington Carver: The Peanut Wizard*. New York: Grosset & Dunlap, 2003.

McKissack, Pat and Frederick McKissack. *George Washington Carver: The Peanut Scientist*. Berkeley Heights, N.J.: Enslow Publishers, 2002.

On the Web

FactHound offers a safe, fun way to find Web sites related to this book. All of the sites on FactHound have been researched by our staff.

1. Visit *www.facthound.com*

2. Type in this special code: 1404837256

3. Click on the FETCH IT button.

Your trusty FactHound will fetch the best sites for you!

Index

Look for all of the books in the Biographies series:

Abraham Lincoln: *Lawyer, President, Emancipator*

Albert Einstein: *Scientist and Genius*

Amelia Earhart: *Female Pioneer in Flight*

Benjamin Franklin: *Writer, Inventor, Statesman*

Cesar Chavez: *Champion and Voice of Farmworkers*

Frederick Douglass: *Writer, Speaker, and Opponent of Slavery*

George Washington: *Farmer, Soldier, President*

George Washington Carver: *Teacher, Scientist, and Inventor*

Harriet Tubman: *Hero of the Underground Railroad*

Martha Washington: *First Lady of the United States*

Martin Luther King Jr.: *Preacher, Freedom Fighter, Peacemaker*

Pocahontas: *Peacemaker and Friend to the Colonists*

Sally Ride: *Astronaut, Scientist, Teacher*

Sojourner Truth: *Preacher for Freedom and Equality*

Susan B. Anthony: *Fighter for Freedom and Equality*

Thomas Edison: *Inventor, Scientist, and Genius*